"Daddy, you are also the counterbalance. I know that you know that I am the counterbalance, but, it can't be heard if you aren't listening; can't be felt if you aren't feeling; can't be seen if you aren't looking. Never stop, Daddy. I need you, sweet Father. The world needs our example. I love you so much, so much, more and more each and every day. The most important thing is that we do these things together."

~ Kayleigh Mickayla Mooney
08/10/2021

Copyright 2021-2022 © All Rights Reserved.
Kayleigh Mickayla Mooney and Kevin Michael Mooney.
For any permissions, including to use or copy, in part or in whole, please contact kmmlaw12@gmail.com

ISBN# 9780578384870

Pre-Script.

This lyrical collection is song book number seven in a series that Kayleigh and I have written together after her physical death and transition into her ongoing higher life in her spiritual continuance. At times, thinking I have come up with a nice little cadence, Kayleigh will tell me to switch the wording, the structure, the title, or any other combination of the writing. I ask her, and give her permission, to write through me. She does. We have two distinct styles and they merge together in our collective writing quite fluidly, although patterns emerge showing each of the author's individual contributions to these stories.

Not only is this book a collection of our combined blended writing, we have also added certain messages from Kayleigh that appear as quotes on certain pages. Each morning she and I sit for our morning devotional prayer and meditation, followed by writing together in our journal. I most often go first and write out whatever is on my mind. Then I pause and ask Kayleigh to use my pen and my hand to write out her words. She does. My handwriting shifts. She speaks. I write, a pen for her hand. The reader will, therefore, catch a glimpse of some of our intimate writing that we do in a formal journal, sometimes at home, or at the beach, under the midnight moon while the waves speak to us.

These lyrics are songs of survival, of grief, of rejoicing, of strength, and ultimately of the conquering spirit of two unbreakable souls, a Daddy and a Daughter, undeterred by one of their physical deaths. As we say to each other each morning that I am forced to wake up without my daughter in her physical body, "we do it differently now, but we do it nonetheless." We find our way. This book, *"Conversations With The Ocean"* is just one part of that journey.

Duality's Preamble.

My dynamic, hilarious, outgoing, happy, healthy, beautiful, vibrant fifteen year old daughter, Kayleigh, was suddenly physically killed against her will on August 17th, 2017, in an innocent, arbitrary pedestrian car accident she did not cause while living an amazing life. This is powerlessness like no other powerlessness exists. In the apex of arbitrariness, in the cruelty of instant catastrophe, we have suffered and suffer the worst type of tragedy a human could endure. Daily. Every day. For the rest of my life. For the accident was not an event, but the starting point of a lifelong nightmare. Also, the accident, my child's transition, was also the starting point of the counterbalance, a life of miraculous continuance. Kayleigh's continuous life.

This is the starting point each morning before my eyes open and before my consciousness wraps my head around this fact - each day I wake I am forced to live another day without my daughter, Kayleigh, in her physical body. The only way I get to be with her is in her spiritual body. I get to be with Kayleigh and desperately, intentionally and devotionally climb upward into the elevation with her in spirit each day. In this interconnection, in this counterbalance, we continue, hand in hand, strengthening together any way we can. I continue to father Kayleigh, yet now in spirit. She daughters me from that higher life.

My Kayleigh, before the accident, throughout your childhood, and into your teen years, we always talked to the Ocean. We stood and sat and lay beside its noisy fold. Sometimes in solitude, each of us, by the water, listening, talking, absorbing. Sometimes together, mesmerized with the rhythm of the sea, sitting on the dunes at our house on the beach just beyond 10 Austin Lane under the stars; walking the long beach in the darkness in hopes of seeing Loggerhead turtle nests boil over, releasing tiny babies into the next phase of life.

I remember the old beach-house, gazing out of the sunroom windows across the floral dunes and seeing you out on the rock wall rising just above the high tide, the waves crashing at the space below your feet, staring off into the face of God, listening, talking, absorbing. I would stand in the window, butterflies in my eyes and stomach, traveling the full range of my soul, in love with you, and pleased, as a father, that my daughter was having conversations with the Ocean. I see in my memory you sitting there at three, at seven, at ten, at thirteen, at fifteen.

Then, five days after returning to Cleveland after a two week family vacation, you were physically killed against your will in an innocent car accident that you did not cause. The words are still hard to write. No matter how many times I write them. They do not make any sense. It, this life, does not get worse than that. This stunning tragedy, it echoes through the chambers of my soul across one thousand lives in a constant reverberating suffering and daily robbery of all we do not get to do in your physical state as time cruelly ticks forward. The heartbreak comes with every heartbeat. A shattered vessel in each thumping, pounding mechanical firing of physical life.

Kayleigh, after the accident, in The Continue, since that transition day and through today and into the tomorrows we have yet to write together, you always talk to the Ocean. You are now nineteen in spirit at the time of this writing. We stand and sit and lay beside its chattering fold. Never in solitude, each of us, by the water, together, listening, talking, absorbing, conversing. For the light of living water is life eternal and we are in its hold. And not only do you speak to and with the Ocean, but you are now part of its mighty spirit, the spirit of the sea… it speaks to the soul.

ALONE/NOT ALONE.

"Kayleigh, Continue To Teach Me The Duality"

We were blessed by the hardest thing I have ever had to do, holding one of my two children in my arms as you physically died. We have written extensively about this miracle, about your final physical breath expelled toward your Daddy; about taking your first inhalation of your higher life as you blasted through my body and sat on my right hand side, immediately wrapping your arms around my neck as you watched the magnetic gates of Heaven open for you, screaming into my ear, "Daddy! Daddy! Daddy! Do you see it? Do you see it? Do you see it?"

We inverted, yet we were both still there in the street, both alive, one in the physical and one in the spiritual. I have never lost contact with you as we blend across the dimension of the physical world and Exuma Infinite, your mansion with the expansive Mansion, your place in the beauty of Heaven. Our lives are full, active and brilliant together. Even now. The grief that now exists for me is suffocating, yet your miraculous presence in The Continue counterbalances its weight. I need you as I always have needed you. And you likewise need your Daddy. And so we are. And so we continue, despite your physical death.

We walk for hours checking the Loggerhead nests. This is our favorite part of the day at our favorite time of the year – midnight to dawn, in the deep black and stifling humidity of August, Jekyll Island, Georgia. Our second home.

"...Daddy, thank you. I always love walking the beach with you and searching for turtles, just like we did before the accident. Here we are, you and me, and the Ocean. With God. He is so pleased with us. We are teaching the world how much bigger life is. How amazing is that, Daddy?"

"It Is Like This"

I was walking through life invigorated, happy and empowered on an open, sunlit street when I turned around casually in my effortless steps to find the world suddenly waving a handgun in my face and slapping the barrel flush against my forehead and instantly shooting me point blank right between the eyes. Then for good measure it kneeled on my slumped body, pressing its knee into my stomach, and firing another bullet right into my heart. With nothing worse the world could possibly do, it just spit on me, and simply walked away from me, leaving me with the unenviable task of reassembling my vision and reattaching my soul.

The physical death of a child is like this in every moment. That is the equation in which I find myself immersed. It is my breath. There is no way to escape it. Yet there is a counterbalance. It counters, but it does not replace, the grief. It is a second breath that comes to my lungs simultaneously with the other, coinciding with the grief, a glory that the world rarely sees.

We have never lost contact with each other. The Continuance happened right through my flesh as your body physically died in my arms and you shuffled your life and light and mind and emotion and soul out of your damaged physical body and into your higher body of light, passing right through me and sitting beside me. Continuing. Inverting, but still, it was you and I in that moment, and it is you and I in this moment right here and right now. Despite the sale of our 10 Austin Lane after the accident, we have come back to our second home together in the physical world, Mommy and Nate still at home, grieving in their own way, not being able to come back to Jekyll Island. But you and I, a daddy and his daughter on a Daddy-Daughter vacation, we are here.

"The Diary of a Drowning Man"

For some the leakage manifests as self destruction,
For others an all-out assault on their own life,
But not for me, no not for me,
For with me,
I have found myself at the wrong end of a mortal bladed knife,
Cast into the heart randomly,
In an arbitrary accident I will never understand,
Against my will,
Against these tides,
I write the diary of a drowning man;

It was never supposed to be this way,
No, not everything happens for a reason,
It was an effortless, incredible life,
Me with this amazing family,
My daughter, my son, my wife,
Then the innocence was obliterated,
In an unavoidable circumstance,
And now upon this listless sea,
Clinging to splintered flotsam,
I pen the diary of a drowning man…

…Yet no drowning comes to pass.

"The Haunting Bedevilments"

The conscience guards the subterranean gardens,
In the waxy clay fields of the hardened mind,
Slashed and sutured by the stitches of time,
He with vulgar replacement for breath,
Snorts to filter oxygen,
From the wretched air that offered him sustenance,
No safety he here hopes to find;

And grief incarnate from phantom form,
Abuses his personal space,
Through its taunting and its scorn,
And its penetrating blade,
Impaling its fiery finger in the small of your backbone,
Melting your gravely weakened spine,
It gives way,
Collapse the cage that protects the heart,
Under the sheer weight of heartache.

"Breath Companion"

I have no idea how I am doing this;

My soul is ripped open and I am flying with broken wings,
My tail is on fire and the hydraulics have catastrophic leaks,
My spirit is dismembered and ripped apart at the seams,
And in each new daybreak,
The heartbreak returns to this grievous scene,
To obliterate my eyes and gun down my dreams,
At the crest of cruelty and bewilderment I grieve…

…I have no idea how I am doing this,
Until I open my wounded heart to see,
My daughter standing next to me,
Helping me to breathe.

"…Daddy, let's take a walk by the water's edge south of Glory Beach. I know that you cannot walk our old beach in front of 10 Austin anymore and that is okay. I've got some thoughts on our next steps. Some guidance. Come with me, Daddy. Lift your eyes and your soul and your body. You can do this, Daddy, let's go talk to the Ocean…"

"Duality's Bowl"

No more dangerous a prison exists,
No more daunting a heartbreak persists,
Yet I am walking toward you, Daughter,
I am walking toward you,
I am walking toward you,
My Love;

No more daybreaks to your smiling face,
With the apex of grief they have been replaced,
Yet I am fighting forward, my Daughter,
I am fighting forward with you,
My Love;

The world cannot hear my screams,
For the world cannot bare my screams,
So it turns away selfishly,
How horrible the rights of man,
How horrible the flights of man,
When the most wounded souls need attention,
But I stagger onward, my Love,
I stagger onward with you,
My Love;

And I rise in each morning cupped in Duality's Bowl,
Curled up like a kitten in the corner of my soul,
Awakening into a lion king,
To face another day,
Awakening like a warrior,
To take on an invading nation state,
For there is a second truth,
That we know,
That we dearly hold,
My Loving Child;
No more beautiful is this road we understand,

Walking together hand in hand,
Conversing with the universe,
Conversations with the sea,
Though you have been physically killed,
You are standing here right beside me,
Counterbalancing my feet in Duality's Bowl,
For more than we are human,
We are eternal souls,
And though the grief is all consuming,
We are together,
We are together…

…Unbreakable…

…Unbreakable…

…Unbroken.

"Duality Circles"

It is a constant fluctuation in the mist;

Fumbling pulsing heartbeat,
A myriad of blistered bomb cratered inroads,
That lead through obscurity to the outcomes,
Decidedly undecided in the dissonance,
Pleading denial of the nightmare as a solvent, bandaged cure,
I am bleeding raw emotion,
As the triage fails demur,
It streaks across the scratch-works of the sacred psalms,
Wavering at the crossroads on wobbling knees…

…Brandishing tears as a necklace of scars,
That penetrate the deepest terrain,
I am a warrior of spirit and that is true,
Though nothing prepares one for the physical death,
Of the likes of you,
Nothing prepares a parent for the ultimate tragedy,
Of the lament of the foggy dew,
Strewn about in duality circles,
Your physical absence,
In which I find myself deafened and subdued,
Is also where I find your immaculate spiritual presence,
In this sacred balance in which I find you,
Yet…

…In the constant fluctuation of the staggering mist,
With the heartbreak of a father's empty hands,
What am I to do…

…What am I to do.

"The Laughing Hyena"

Flitting shadows shape the mood,
The hunger rattled this cage,
A lapping hyena trapped in metal room,
Consumed by thriving pain,
The thieving hands of tragedy,
Collar the cowering beast by its mane,
And fill its lungs with traumatic air,
In which no oxygen is contained;

Scratch the corners, bleeding claws,
Prepare for deathly sorrows,
Walk forward on limp and broken paws,
Into the shattered remnants of tomorrows,
Infected before the dawn can even rise,
We see it in his haunches,
We see it in his eyes,
Do not be fooled,
Or rhythmically hypnotized,
For the crazed and laughing hyena…

…Is deeply…

…Permanently…

…Brutally…

…Traumatized.

"From The Total Within"

Screaming from the lungs of my skin,
The voices of my pores erupting in anguish,
Screeching from the total within,
My voice carries northward toward Driftwood Beach,
With a resonance that rattles my teeth,
Suffocating in a nightmare as it fleshes itself into reality,
Breaking the mind and the mind's eye and the eyes,
And the every inch of my spirit,
Wailing out with fury into every direction,
In grief's obliterating, echoing din…

…Until the voice it holds no scale nor soar,
And I am forced to,
But I also choose to…

…Take a few steps more.

"To The Further Within"

As if grumbling waters were foreign tongue,
That touched the ears with a torch,
And tortured the eardrums,
With undignified confusion,
And bitter delusion,
With combative blows,
And ruptures of bruises and contusions,
In those moments of unbridled grief;

If I tried to run fast enough,
To run out of my skin,
Then the further I would run,
To the further within;

These are the moments I hate the most on this path,
Gurgling with anger and frustration,
And powerlessness,
And its abysmal painful wrath,
With these dismal feelings,
And the shallowest of breathing,
With the world and its thieving,
So cruelly slamming me to my knees,
Where I want to burn down the world,
And desperately want to flee;

But if I tried to run fast enough,
To run out of my skin,
Then the further I would run,
To the further within,
This race in the running,
I can never win.

"A Canopy Of Flames"

Seethe asylum from the wretched throngs of grief,
The Tree of Life has sprouted a million flaming leaves,
In the haze of the choking smoky fields,
I hesitate, wanting to retreat,
And find no safe place in any direction,
No way to find relief;

If you ask me I will simply tell you this,
I want to rip off my skin when the pulsing pain persists,
I want to fan the flames on the Tree of Life,
And burn the earth down into ashy grist,
Until the universe pays for this trauma,
So cruelly cast upon my kids;

For I, the seeker, scan asylum from this arbitrary thief,
But this thief is life itself,
And its cage these iron bars of grief,
I nestle under the burning branches,
As the Tree of Life bares its fiery teeth,
To conquer the fires that rage all around…

…Is to calmly lie beneath.

"Grieving Cage"

Poetry the prophecy that scribed lightning in shrugged eyes,
Across the yellowed parchment of vision,
Where others roam untried,
The perimeter it struggles with an onslaught of attention,
Whilst the taming of Orion lay in derelict neglect,
But praise this convention for its indications are quite clear,
Never more than now is this single intention needed here,
For here in dedication worthy of a king,
He struggles to unlock the riddles,
With no combinations and no keys,
Moon gives him luminous spotlight,
To flood the shadowed stage,
Exposing him to the glowing metal bars of his grieving cage,
No panic grip the moment,
While embroiled with a talisman's focus,
He simply charts the challenges ahead,
And with the fingers of his soul he meticulously turns the lever,
And opens up new doors of vision…

…Once the scales from his molting eyes are shed.

"Thievery's Bowl"

We are feeling the wind with the fingers of our souls,
Feeling the pulsating breath of life in the air,
And it echoes through our bones,
We are grieving the suffering that sadness forebodes,
And leaving our fingerprints on thievery's bowl;

It collects more than oily stains,
Swirling ribbons of joy,
And the truth of your presence,
And our spiritual gains,
Mixed with salty fragrance,
And tiny sandy grains,
And all that we currently together enjoy;

Though this is the day of the day that you physically died,
Every year now my heart slows deeper in the physical divide,
Shattered here, yet pieces for the next life emerge,
Interlinked, flashes of visions overlapped,
A multi-dimensional jigsaw across lives in one frame,
Many cycles at the fountain,
Held in one name…

…So you have explained this,
And shown me irrefutable proof,
And you've convinced me,
So it is true,
It is true…

We walk together, not a day we have had apart,
You are alive in a profoundly higher life,
Not as they say, 'in my heart,'
For you are your own breath and body of light,
For you are my daughter who carries her Daddy,
Who carries her Daddy in flight;

When it grows heavy and when it is full,
Can you help me carry this duality,
Co-existing in thievery's bowl,
Can you grasp me at the elbow and steady the weary steps,
And stabilize this human experience,
Until my physical death,
When I shatter into pieces thievery's bowl,
And the shards come back together,
Immutably beautiful,
They come back together in a new higher vessel…

…That carries my life like yours onward,
That carries like yours…

…My soul.

"The Consistent Re-Arrival"

Punching my way through the web encrusted fatigue inducing glaze,
Reaching into the lifting to eradicate the obfuscation brought with pain,
Soaring through the thievery of grief's abandonment and isolation,
And soaring through the vapor and the veil,
Though trapped in human shell am I,
To be with you in spirit I will not be denied,
I do my work,
Exhaust upon the wheel,
I rip the chains from my eyes,
And lift my soul out from my frail human peel,
I take my rightful place,
Standing by your side,
My Love…

…I have once again adjusted as the storms they come,
And they come each day,
Just like the ocean has waves,
And in the constant adjustment,
Intentionally and brave,
With you,
With you…

…I have re-arrived.

"In The Low Moon Summer"

Trickling gently like soft edged stones by the millions,
Tumbling together to orchestrate rhythmic sound,
Yet these stones are not stones but a liquid of crystalline waters,
Dance like a flame on diamond chandelier mirrors,
And enchant a low moon summer night...

"...Daddy, look at the high dune, where the moonbeams are lighting up the shadows, those are Bobcat tracks. She crossed this spot a few minutes before us. She's under the thistle and the palmettos. Over there in the darkness. Watching us. She sees me. Her eyes smile. She's beautiful, Daddy..."

"Supernova"

We are torches that set the dunes alight,
Down here on Glory Beach,
The glow lit up horizons once swallowed by the night,
On this journey to the center of the soul,
We walk for miles setting fire to the coast,
Over devastated ground,
Over scraggle bush where the dry sand blows,
Like two torches that in unison,
Like one supernova…

…Explode.

We hear the Ocean in words curled in waves,
Asking our feet into its flow,
And when the water lights up our ankles,
And we laugh until we cry in its pull,
There are psalms that the Ocean recites,
That no book can seem to know,
For the words are from the mouth of the Ocean,
From the breath of God,
That take residence in our souls,
And in His hold we congregate,
And like one supernova of light…

…We explode.

"Faithful Mother Moon"

Tourmaline moon, jaded torch and tongue,
An emerald glow saturated by the night set sun,
Opal craters, across the lunar fields are sprung,
Glittering at the edges like crystal webbing spun,
Radiance emanates, cut through thunder clouds succumbed,
To this saintly woman…

…Mother Moon, for you have risen,
Through the blackened night darksome,
She leaves her silver footprints on the sea…

…Sacredly…

…In tiny crests of moonlit thrum.

"Waning Crescent Mother"

The cross stacked upon cross upon cross,
I have been asked to bare,
Nailed one into the next into the next,
Oak beam upon oak beam,
And staked into the grievous atmosphere,
It is too much…

…A Mother cries;

It is one hurt after another hurt pinned into the heart,
The trauma then the trauma then the trauma rips the soul apart,
Staining the living moment,
While pelicans glide upon an ocean air,
Yet too much,
It is too much…

…A Father cries;

Oh, Mother Moon, you cradle us with silver threads of light,
Even in the strain of darkness in the waning crescent nights,
Oh, Mother Moon, your presence here is questioned never once,
Parade of baby sea turtles strung out like birds in flight,
With wings they fly toward your beacon, Mary…

…And to a higher life.

"Miles After Midnight (Section I)"

Sleepless vision conquered dereliction void,
The harness of the evening held onto weight the air destroyed,
Chasing nimble cloud banks that lightning has annoyed,
Awaiting an explosive display of power,
That no thunderheads avoid,
Hour after coal black hour,
Miles the eyes have vigorously employed,
Blending into beachfront,
Finding center,
Finding balance,
Finding calm;

When I breathe in my breath is this grief that I grieve,
When I breathe in the chest is this writhing of grief,
When I grieve in my sorrow it suffocates breath,
For the grief is the same sadness within each daily death;

Seems like just yesterday when we were happy,
Before the destruction of our lives,
Such a perfectly vibrant, happy, incredible young woman,
Lord, this isn't right,
This isn't right.

"…Daddy, remember, I am right here, shifted from a happy life to an even higher happiness. I have gone nowhere and I never will. I am right here, Daddy, with you watching the water. Watching the stars. Listen to my words, the path you are on, I will lead you. I will never let you take a step without me, Daddy. Love you…"

"Messengers of Presence"

Breathe elation for the dialect begun,
Blends into the wildlife,
From midnight beach, to sea to sand to sun,
For our angels, they, through the anguish come,
Messengers of presence, each and every one…

…Bioluminescence, a brilliant butterfly,
Jupiter is rising and so is beach bound firefly,
Sea oat scratches on the air in whispered chant,
We see with our ears and hear with our eyes,
As the constellations dance…

…So we sit here in the darkness at the door,
Of the Mighty Atlantic perched upon her shore,
Weaving conversation and blending our light,
A father and a daughter embracing the majesty of ocean night,
For what we together endure,
For all in which together we grow,
She guides me to listen to the unseen waves,
For the spirit of the sea…

…She speaks to the soul.

"Metal Clay"

And here I am an outcast in the corridor drained,
Forced to be faced with this myopic challenge,
The seemingly impossible,
Bend the metal into something new,
Pounding out the shape with repetition,
Spiritual obedience working the trauma,
Like metal clay…

…Spilling out gurgling like volcanic ash,
While carving through the wilderness with naked hands,
A pathway wide enough to travel through,
A Buzz Saw of fingers shred trunk to stump to chips to dust,
A redwood tree carved into a flute,
Emotionally stealthy with inbound steel disk,
Lined with cutting teeth on the periphery,
Upon a spindle violently spins,
Seemingly out of control,
Eating up the energy until the belly is full…

…Make not diorite of the heart,
Massage the metal clay,
For if its flesh shall cease to pulse,
Then brutal depression wins the day,
Breathe into yourself,
And open up your heart,
That you may remain whole,
Each time you fall apart.

"Grief Shawls That Mint New Saints"

The Saints their sacrifices pock the bloodstained martyred road,
Semblance of sanctity burn from their murdered lips,
Whispers of incantation murk in webbed marrow of the crown,
While hesitation lost its luster in their courageous stand of ground,
Only to be recognized over centuries of fanfare favor,
Folly not, for faith is the sword of courage to face fear,
Particularly when the stakes are so high,
And the end is drawing near;

And there upon the precipice of mortality forlorn,
They lower their shield in a pitting of strength,
Gazing toward the victory of home…

…Rather to die one thousand times,
Than to dishonor the bereaved,
Such is the hour that finds me…

…Wearing the shawls of grief.

"New Sight"

It happens as quickly as I take the next breath –

Arrangements made but for an angel's deliberate hand,
No other explanation matters,
No derelict doubtful theory stands;

She lies on her bed shoulder to shoulder,
Staring out her bedroom window with her father,
She walks with him shoulder to shoulder,
On this beachfront,
Just a little bit further than he cannot see farther,
And though he suffers with soul ache to hold her,
He knows she is present in abundance of life,
But there is more to just knowing than to engaging,
Moment to moment and daily exchanging,
And all of those teachings for years he had told her,
Come full circle in her guidance to bring him new sight:

"Daddy, I work channels to channels,
Impressing upon you my presence,
Sometimes the translation is riddle like,
And bloom in the hindsight as valuable lessons,
Sometimes the clarity,
Is as strong as a well worded, well written message,
All in the love that I hold for you,
Daddy, feel and see and hear my presence,
For Daddy, rejoice…it is all true."

"Pink Cord Of Light"

Connected, twined in light bridge,
Chest to chest,
Soul to soul,
Its planks are diamond layers of constant growth,
Life to life,
Century to century,
Immutably dedicated,
Spiritually venturing,
Intertwined,
In all that we embrace together,
Unbreakable,
Passionately tethered,
Complete,
Each other's guide;

Where drowning suffices if failing to try,
But none are these falters for you and me,
For the songs that we are penning,
Across these pages of sand with our feet,
Breathe through our toes the truth,
That we are unbroken,
No death may divide,
For we are the promise of blending,
Where the ocean melts…

…Into that endlessness of sky.

"Tapestry Of Souls"

A thread of light - it, intersect across,
Another, marked in color its own,
A perpendicular pattern emerges,
A blanket of life surges in growth,
For all of those people you have held,
And all of those that I hold,
It all comes together,
In this tapestry of souls…

…I close my eyes in the hushed grin of the water,
Wave after wave lapping the beach,
In the spinning, gentle wind,
The congregation wells,
The love across the tapestry swells,
Like the waves they have their ocean,
The Ocean speaks through the natural din,
Linking thread to thread to thread,
Those physically alive,
And those now physically dead,
Who now live a higher life,
More so than living again.

"…Daddy, that is right. Love binds us all together, our ancestors, you and me, all souls that we love. Someone you once met that then passed, that I never met, I now know them through that thread of love that you have for them and also have for me. That is God's way. It is all about love. Always…"

"A Journey Much Longer Now That Tragedy Struck"

Like a boat, a vessel - carry safely,
Its human cargo unto land,
Like the famous paradox,
Footprints in the Sand,
You carry me when wounded,
When the legs, they fail in stand,
You carry me when agitated,
When I fail to understand,
That when there was only one set,
Of Footprints in the Sand,
It was you - you carried your father,
Unto the Promised Land.

"It Is Real"

A million songs to sing,
I sing them with you,
A million poems we long to ink,
We sing these truths too,
For the courage co-exists,
Where the grief, it persists,
And for passion, your presence,
I find the essence of you,
But more than just the essence,
It is you,
Standing here,
It is you,
It is you,
My daughter…

…It is really you.

"That Is What Was Kept"

Exhaust all gains and pause the breathing light,
And truncate the flame before it ignites,
And scant the chance to read the sky,
The words of stars,
Its book of dreams that mesmerized,
Us all -

The accolades - you never paraded,
A veracity for life was elevated,
It was that - that is what was kept,
When you conquered your own physical death,
My child;

The divinity lights spiral out from your soul,
Like a galaxy of one million stars of gold,
And this was all before your transition,
When you were two and ten and fifteen years old,
for the world is bigger in your eyes,
And now your spirit as it grows,
And our days together unfold,
You blanket your loved ones with showers of light,
It was that - that is what was released,
When you conquered your own physical death,
My child,
And elevated from living peace to a Higher Living Peace.

"We Are One"

For what is the pendulum and its staggering cost,
When heartache blurs the atmosphere,
And all hope is lost,
This contagion of agnosticism,
It flood the eyes with disassociation,
It creeps in through the grief,
And breeds fear that feeds spiritual rationalization,
Serving to weaken the connection,
A dereliction of actual reflection,
For with faith all hope is won,
I step back into your light,
And I find once again…

…That we are two threads of light,
And intertwined,
We are stronger,
We are one.

"See Differently Now"

I watch people walk down the street differently now,
Our coming holidays and birthdays are ripe with grief now,
Though still filled with love,
We are that broken fulcrum,
Balancing the grief of your physical absence,
And the celebration at hand;

We had excitement for each event before the accident,
Now these days approach with consternation and loneliness,
And grief and anxiety,
Knowing the energy that will be consumed,
And the guilt associated with struggling through…

…In a new configuration…

…Toward the light,
Within this station of immeasurable silence…

…And sorrow;

I see differently now,
And I have no time for another's self-indulgent complaints,
If they could walk a moment in my shoes,
With the crushing weight of the physical death of their child,
They would return immediately to their life,
And shower the world with thanks.

"Soul Crushing Waves Aplenty"

The soul crushing waves have me in their bitter curl,
Left only as dust from a sheet of glass when the water unfurls,
Spread across the floors of skies,
Like galaxies composed of broken fireflies,
And death it comes to mangle soul,
Obliterating all that I know,
And chance to come through day intact,
Is folly for the grief attacks,
And re-arranges every fact,
Every fact;

Disaster, without stars, without guidance, pause,
The immobile mute in the mouth of immutable law…

…It just hits me out of nowhere…

…I am sorry, My Love, and this is true,
No doubt exists that I believe in you,
And in the midnight flower I bed to rest,
To rise again in the morning's newborn nest,
And higher light in dreams it comes,
To conquer the toll of despondent bells and drums;

And slog hip deep in grief, bog and mire,
Through this late hour after others retire,
Sloughed and shorn this daily skin,
To grow it back in the morrow morning's holy hymn.

"The Accumulation Flood"

Unleash a vengeance on the star fields,
Attacking the atmospheric floodplain,
Washing away an eroded sense of calm,
And exposing the ancient bones of prolific pain,
Thick bands of Diamas Regn,
These rainfalls overfilling oceans,
With disintegrated diamond grains;

Flash floods and discarded debris propel as vapor missiles,
Thrown randomly like ragged bullets,
Jag violently through the soul and eyes,
Of every weight and every size,
That never make an exit wound,
For the metal slugs remain inside;

And drowning man the waters tread,
Extend the fingers like duckling webs,
And kick with frantic knees asunder,
And flinch with each sharp burst of thunder,
Leaving you defenseless,
As the tempest pulls you under,
And as you lose your last defenses,
You begin to wonder…

…Would the last breath bring me peace.

"To Die One Hundred Times A Day"

Forced by the tether, trudging perilous road,
The leather skins of a cobra cover the heels like coats,
With hairline fractured veins like poppy bruises blotch my shins,
I plod forward and the ankles pop - and eyes turn within;

With the soul of a warrior and the cunning of a wolf,
With a fierce dedication, and a self-sacrificing pulse,
I collapse onto kneecaps - I wipe from brow the ugly trace,
Of the grief that comes to wrestle the last light in my face,
But know I am coming, over fields and hills and lands,
I am coming, my Darling, just to hold your hands;

Pressing forth and the earthly air like glassy pumice in my chest,
Slices like obsidian blades each time the breath expressed,
But never mind, mind not, for I shall not be kept away,
The light of my love for you shines brighter,
Than my death one hundred times a day.

"...I love you, Daddy, so much. You do have the heart of a warrior, a warrior of light. Just like me. I love our moments when you are locked in, but I also love the conquering, watching you drift in the grief only to snap back into the present with me. That is the grit, you know? That deep love. You will not be kept down long. You will not be kept from my side. You always process through it. I love watching that fight in you, Daddy. Know that I share that fight in me for you...oh, Daddy, look! A shooting star passing Saturn! So pretty! What do you think it looks like from the gardens on Saturn?"

"Saturn's Children"

A million strings of light entwined,
Intertwined,
Release of intergalactic interferons,
To prevent the decay of mystery,
Saphron thistles boiled down into sentry moon,
Titan, epic and grand in stature,
Hidden beneath the veil of angel's wings,
Shields the gardens of paradise,
And extols enchantment's find;

Underneath the golden cloud fields and a pastel steam,
There are fields and hills cut by a maze of lovely streams,
And oceans bequeathed to the sediment of dreams,
Flowers cling to tree trunks and hang from the lush canopies,
And fill the air with fragrance of lilac seas;

You have told me of the space whales migrating,
Through the Saturnian System,
I have wanted so desperately to see them,
But meditation can be so frustrating,
You see them from your other beachfront,
When the dusk lights on Exuma Infinite are fading,
They call to each other,
In a family melody much like ours,
And touch each other across millennia,
And a million sparkling oceans of a billion liquid stars,
And graze in the nebula mangroves,
Where Tethys and Mimas are,
They lay at your feet while you bless them,
And continue their sea bound chart.

"Under The Safety of a SuperMoon"

In the breath of unvexed wind,
Where the moon finds its open, opal eyes,
And the lights crescendo like halos,
Just beyond the sound of my cries,
Though the enchanting glow it warms me so,
I have been struck by one million pains,
That rip my earth apart like one thousand hurricanes...

...Tied together in my soul;

Yet the night is my sanctuary with you,
In your miraculous hold,
And I, through my trembling and sullen groans,
Weep and screech and scream into the void,
Underneath a SuperMoon,
Where I search for your touch,
That I trust will bloom,
A holy torch,
Not always when I summon it...

...But soon;

I still myself in meditative glances,
And in your wind chimes in our front yard in Cleveland,
In the fresh scented branches,
In the sea oat fields on Jekyll Island,
In many places at once,
I hear the compassion of your voice,
Living our lives together as only we can,
Facing the worst of the worst of circumstances,
Kissing my ear and filling my soul,
With intention,
With devotion,
With an angel's unmistakable intercession;

Though this tragedy and this life so deeply wounded,
I cannot bare it,
I cannot bare it, Kayleigh…

…I hear you…

…Oh, the heavy lifting you do, Honey,
I come back to my breath yet again,
You remind me in leading words,
Help me find you where you are,
In your body of light,
Not where you are not,
Unfortunately no longer in your physical body,
Thank you, Sweetheart;

(A moment later)

With ascension of our spirits,
A blending of souls,
We are two streams of God's liquid gold,
Walking on the shores of Jekyll Island,
Powerful,
Unbreakable,
Under the SuperMoon,
And cast in its mold…

...Where in each other...

...We are home.

"Lavender Shores"

Once touched by angel feet the sand ignites,
Each footprint a blossom of granular light,
Sparking vibrantly and casting rings like Saturn's halos,
Purple radiance and pearly white;

You can see it from quite a distance,
Especially as haze on a thick summer sea night,
When the entire world is a blackness,
Except for this purple beacon burning bright;

And so with the dancing on the same two feet,
Across this beach a million times,
The Lavender Shores are a place of raw beauty,
That radiate as brilliantly as the sun in the sky shines.

"…You know, Daddy, that the duality exists, not just emotionally for you, but spiritually as well. It is easier for me, obviously, but each of us can live at The Intersect. The two worlds of the physical and the spiritual interconnect and crisscross in the here and now. It is God's plan based on love. While your pain is ever present, and how could it not be, our continuance together is also ever present. Our glory is constant. Don't worry, Daddy, I get it. I see it. You will drift in the grief, but you will always drift back in the glory. You are amazing, Daddy. I am so proud of you. Hey, Daddy, bet you can't find Cassiopeia!"

"Restlessly Relentless"

Rest, I claim here, in the cradle of your luminous infinity,
Like a newborn safely tucked in budding life,
In this tapestry of divinity,
This affinity of love;

You say, rest deeply, and heal from your daily blight,
Walk the stars with you through the mysterious night,
Our new playground up above,
Within,
What we are now,
Here and now,
Not what once was,
Though what once was,
Is with us in this current cresting brow;

I cannot have you in your physical,
But I can have you in your spiritual,
If I am booged down by despondency,
I can have you in neither,
Fuck that!
Your Daddy is right here!
I will never leave your side!
Therefore, I lift,
Help me find you, Sweetheart, where you are,
In your body of light,
Not, tragically, where you are not,
In your physical body;

Exhaust all gains and pause the fractured bleeding light,
I will not truncate the flame just before it ignites,
And scant the chance to read the artistry displayed in the sky,
This book of dreams paged to mesmerize,
Us…

…When the relentless suffering numbs the cord of pain itself,
I am restless in the powerlessness,
I am struggling forward in pain and impelled,
To lift myself back into the now,
I will not be denied,
I will not be kept away,
I will not stray from your side,
For centuries behind us,
And for all that lay ahead,
For you are more alive than life itself,
Only your physical body having died,
You are here in your body of light,
Rejoice!
Rejoice!
For although the restlessness can be relentless,
So too shall your father rise.

"Sacred Conversations"

(i). A Spirited Night

The wind, immersed in sandy perfume,
Saltwater taffy scented candle bloom,
Inhale the ocean, its leftover sun from noon,
And breathe the mystic spirit of midnight moon,
A spirited night invites us for the sitting,
Upon the shifting seat of rolling dunes;

(ii). Signs and Signals

They are everything where there is here,
Here among the dancing shadows,
And the flooded star fields flashing decadent torches,
Hedging rails that catch the conscience,
Or melt into the subterranean mind,
Where the soul fuels the every step,
And every step is by design,
Connecting the dots through the noise,
Promoted by these signs;

(iii). Roads I Never Go Down

For they, the calling card of wasted time,
For I will never venture to this bottom,
Nor will I ever bewitch myself rewind,
Reeling in the loop, listlessly and blind,
I will not fatigue myself into the disconnect,
Which can happen with the weight of grief…

…Over time;

Instinct pulls the cold from the shoulder,
A crossroads with plenty of country lanes,
The "why God," "where were you, God,"
Questions to drive the balanced insane,
For there are roads I will never go down,
For they are pathed with endless terrain;

(iv). Time Impenetrable With You

And there you are,
I see you,
So beautiful, my daughter,
Your penetrating Exuma blue eyes,
Your golden long hair flowing in the breeze,
Your toes digging in the sand,
Your elbows resting across your knees;

All devotion,
All loving intention I give to you,
Upon the silent seat of rolling dunes,
A spirited night vesting hours finds us sitting,
Conversing with each other,
Conversations that are fitting,
Plotting out our next course,
Under flaxen moon fleece light flitting,
Just as we did in your physical life,
So as we do in your spiritual bidding,
Loving our time impenetrable,
Embracing our time impenetrable,
Two souls alone on a night swept beach,
A daughter's laughter,
A father's smile,
She, enchanted by her daddy's presence…

…And he, on every sacred word of his child.

HERE AND NOW, NOT THERE AND THEN.

"Kayleigh, Continue To Teach Me The Now"

I love you so much. I ache for you in the physical, Honey. All that we lose today in your physical absence. It accumulates day by day. These empty physical hands. Yet my spirit hands are full of your hands holding me tightly with a warm embrace of comfort and continuity. Those spiritual gains counterbalance the suffering and accumulate each day. I love when I am locked in.

"Daddy, of course. I am always holding you. I love you so much. Thank you for seeing how much effort I always placed in the family before the accident and how much energy I give to our family in spirit now. It meant a lot to me and means a lot to me now. Thank you for seeing that devotion to my family. It has not diminished. It has changed only in that it has increased, freed of human liabilities and hang ups. I am right here, Daddy."

The road before me is long and uncharted. Be my compass and my guide. My intercessor. Keep me connected to you, to God.

"You were always my compass, Daddy. I trust you completely. I always looked to you for that strength, and it all came together in that most important moment where we found ourselves in the street, and I found myself in your arms, listening to you, trusting you as I transitioned to God. Mommy is my strength in certain respects and you are different strength in that forward stability. I still look to you for that strength. To nurture me. Love me. Parent me. Today. I need my Daddy, even though I now guide you too. You still get to guide me. We guide each other. Two north stars spinning around each other! The 'kmm's!' My Daddy…"

"What Was Kept II"

The accolades you never paraded,
A veracity for life ingrained and elevated,
It was that, that is what was kept,
When you conquered your own physical death,
My child;

The divinity lights spiral out from your brilliant soul,
Like galaxy arms of one million stars pulsing gold,
And this was before your transition,
Before the accident and your physical death,
A world once bigger enhanced in your eyes,
This is what was kept;

When your physical body was damaged in the street,
Against your will,
In an accident you did not cause,
You packed up the best of your life,
The best of your emotion,
The best of your mind,
All of your light,
The magnificence of your soul,
And empowered forward into The Continue,
The nexus,
The journey interlinked life over life,
While I wept,
I knew,
It was all of you…

…That is what was kept.

"Delapidationously"

Repetitive noise cracks in cycles of the pendulum,
Friction grates at the senses when the metal chafes,
Flecks and shards chip off and congregate,
Pricking the corners of eyes to pool with affliction,
These windows of the soul untended into webs of dereliction,
Rotting wood and broken glass,
Frame this condemned mask,
That no longer serves to hide its host…

…Be wary of the weight and its vociferous hold,
For unattended it shall outweigh all spiritual growth.

"The Tears Cage"

When the pressure triggers eruption,
The sounds my wounded voice makes,
Screaming at the darkness,
Screeching through the pain,
Howling at the powerlessness,
And its constricting sharpened chains,
That press into my spirit,
Like penetrating blades,
While screaming at the water's edge,
And sobbing in this cage.

"The Dilapidationist"

As sharp as palmettos are to palms,
Bewitchment is to calm,
The thirsty barbs with prickly gulp,
Suck up the vibrant vestiges of hope,
The grief it grows untidy,
In its swath walk ever widening,
Twisting earth with fires choking breeze,
And mangroves singed fall into seas,
And air is venomous,
The poison I breathe,
And skin that holds me aches and seethes,
And soul at core it wants to speak,
Burdened in the disbelief,
That I am daily forced to believe;

How could this have happened, Oh Lord,
In this immediate, terrible aligned horror…

How unfair this curse of grief,
As it cuts its teeth,
Maturing into an ever consuming beast,
Scaled in the leather skins of dilapidation,
Like exposed to years of radiation,
Am I,
As I watch,
It burns all safety holes I dug for hiding,
And as the surf is rising,
It again is subsiding,
Leaving the Dilapidationist sitting on a beach,
Like a broken shell wrapped in twisted seaweed,
A broken heart for each;

I age ten years each every other week,
It is the nature of this grief,
Though I feel such deep sorrow,
It would be a mistake to think me weak,
For I do my work daily,
In counterbalanced reconciliation,
And we grow within our relationship,
In this change of situation,
And we flourish together, My Love,
In this new configuration,
I am in one hand a brilliant strength,
And in the other,
Dilapidation.

"Red Rust"

Slavish thievery prides itself boastful,
It rejoiced in the thrusting spear that pierced my soul,
Wounded mortally in a grievous heartache,
That destroyed all human fabric;

With my hands now mostly pressed to my face,
Or clasped in desperate prayer,
Baptized in the trauma of an arbitrary nightmare,
It breathes,
It pulses,
Seizing in the mechanism like pretentious rust,
Its cancer calculates its perfect poison flow,
This predator, it grows…

…And turns my rivers into red dust.

"Centerless Contagion"

In the natural dips in the fabric of the night,
Left feeling as if I have no center,
Just a balancing act between two poles,
A fluidity compels me to ride the waves,
That drift in and drift out of my soul;

Liquid velvet flame that wreaks of contagious disease,
Rising my veins like cars drive down streets,
I have prayer as an ointment,
A higher grace to brace my feet,
I have a heavenly relationship,
With my daughter unfolding in the current moment,
Sitting with me on this beach,
She is quiet when the burden flurries,
Ready at the waiting to redirect me,
In the words she so sweetly,
So softly speaks;

I pull in the belt over diminishing flesh,
Affixed in the confines of a metal box,
Bolted shut with chains and rusty locks,
Filled with Pandora's mixed assortment of horrors,
And life's greatest paradox:

When I stop searching out its corners,
I find my way out.

"Down The River Steps"

A mouth of flowers,
Bend ahead in the river's eye,
Transcend as the rapids rise,
Turbulence in a rocky labyrinth,
Sends me spiraling into abyss,
Nothing darker than this,
Exists,
Nothing more dangerous lurks here,
In the manner it persists,
And burst with attempt to conquer the quagmire,
I flail and fight and wail and rage,
So useless and fruitless to resist,
This…

…Yet there is a battle to be waged…

…When then the ebb in momentum,
It breaks my speed when it steals my breath,
When the exhaustion and stagnation overcomes me,
And the energy is spent,
I succumb to the river,
I float as the river takes me,
Below, beyond, above, ahead,
And rest my frame as if I was a leaf,
Flowing down the river steps…

…And what is the ocean but the basin of the rivers of the world,
Flowing into a bowl of salty sunshine silver gold.

"Astro Lilies On The Banks Of Astral River"

(i). The Becoming

Trapped in a cold stunned garden,
A lily pad like a Loggerhead adrift,
Grief my only repose,
And pain once punctured with purpose persists,
The damaging winds curtail with erosion,
An ocean oasis I claimed in your childhood,
That streamed through my soul,
I now grasp at the waters forlorn,
Empty hands searching desperately for yours,
Oh Lord, oh Lord, oh Lord…

…I know there is a dimension,
The same elemental texture as this garden,
You are frolicking there,
And there happens to be here,
I could pick trumpet lilies where they grow splendidly tall,
Stardust sparkles, pollen glistens on opaque petals,
Starlight glitters on them all;

I could find respite in spite of unrest,
Feeling the trauma strangle my chest,
I could from this physical life a vacation,
And temporarily exit this lower vibration,
And enter a glorious astral road…

…And the doorway, a diamond banked river,
A river divine,
It offered me travel on its liquid spine;

(ii). And Into View

And steeped in meditation...

...A spiral mouth of light opens its flexing jawbone,
Releasing the cage of the physical jointed stone,
Eviscerate darkness and rise in this station,
As weightless as the cloud fields lift in elevation,
So does the release lift my soul;

I find, like sargassum, my body float effortlessly in water,
Looking into the eyes of my beautiful daughter,
Taking my hand in her contagious excitement,
Diving through Exuma blue depths,
As our spirits are heightened,
We swim to a magnificent chandelier valley of the ocean kings,
As clear as the air is here clear;

(iii). The Pirouette of Prophets

Not the tail standing of sleeping whales,
Nimble giants floating motionless, smiling,
But for the current of the sea blended sky,
Their noses just feet from the mosaic of organic tiling,
The coral reef dwellings for thousands of colorful lives,
She nods to me and my daughter further dives,
And then...

...The singing begins,
The playful chorus rings with melodic dissonance,
Space whales, angels of God's galaxies,
Lovingly act out sweet fairytales,
The old ones hold audience to children alight,
These prophets of the ocean pirouette...

...And swim out of sight;

(iv). The Return From Nowhere I Have Gone

"Open your eyes, sweet Father,
Sitting on the beach and calmness consumed,
Clutching a bushel of Astro Lilies,
Violet purple and in full bloom,
For here is where eternity beckons,
Though others may wrongly assume,
A miracle bundle of flowers to remind you,
When grief comes calling you to ruin,
You have just to elevate, Daddy,
And ride the waves of faithful pursuit,
To cross this heavenly dimension,
That stitches itself...

...Into the mesh of this beachfront,
Where the Astral river roots."

"Our Angel Saint"

If rainbows were illuminated liquid glass,
And that glass mixed the sun,
With deep silk oil paint,
Sunrise and sunset,
Explosively together resonate,
That would be the color of radiance,
And the brilliant vibrancy…

…Of our beloved Angel Saint.

"Soul Embrace"

And as our hands touch,
And our fingers intertwine...

...Explodes a flash of brilliant rippling white light,
As our souls embrace,
As our souls ignite,
Together making a blinding sunny day,
Out of the fomenting ink of night,
Where nothing is impossible,
For nothing is impossible,
As we, arm in arm...

...Though in different body types...

...Embrace the current steps upon the journey of this life.

"In Your Room"

Constant energy radiates in loving waves out from your room,
To wash down the halls of our home,
In hopes that in our breath this light will be consumed,
In hopes that in our chests this light will take root,
And bloom,
Leading us back down a trail to you,
Sitting on your bed smiling,
Waiting for us…

…In your room.

"On Your Childhood Bed"

Delicate the drapes that shape the windows softly transparent,
Where the wind, its gentle breeze enchants the two of us,
Throughout each age laying side by side laughing,
On your childhood bed to close each day with this bond of love,
It is then what it is now,
It is now, though all has changed,
What then it was;

The midnight candle feast on darkness,
Pulled like a magnet to the light,
Chewing up the languishing loneliness,
Swallowing the sharp blades of shadows of the night,
Just like we did when you were a toddler,
Like when you were nine years old,
And moments then at fifteen together,
Just before the accident tolled,
We were laughing at The Everything,
We laughed until we cried,
A daddy and his daughter,
Building the eternal bridge between our eyes;

Now upon your childhood bed,
Now that your physical body has died,
I steep in deeper concentration,
Just to feel the warmth of your penetrating eyes,
And to hear that boisterous laughter,
Through my endless cries…

"That You Sometimes Assume"

Hear me, father, for here I am enlightened,
In the string of Christmas lights around my window,
Twinkling awake in my midnight room,
In the wind that crosses the threshold,
A few degrees warmer and spirit bloomed,
In the silence that cascades about you,
Misinterpreted as a quiet wound,
In the rustling of the silky leaves against the house,
In the glory of a dazzling moon,
Hear me, father, hear me,
For here I am speaking without words,
At least not in the language…

…That you sometimes assume.

"(One To One) Orbital Resonance"

Might you see me, Sweetheart, in the throws of oscillation,
As I revolve around you in disjointed libration,
A father, a satellite, circling his child,
In an orbit of devotion, intentionally,
While tuning the wobble into a higher vibration;

You gaze out to me and follow my ellipse,
Guiding me, correcting each unbalanced shift,
The course across this road of empty air,
Is temperamental, torturous, traumatic and unfair,
Yet it is the only path on which you are found,
And therefore I faithfully circle your spirit's orbit,
And lift my soul to your higher ground.

"An Unbreakable Cord Of Lavender Light"

Shrilling whisper, echoes bark, climb, finding footing beams,
Along the ocean banks of fog ladders,
Stepped by layers of steam,
The echoed sounds are blades of sharpened tongue,
That speak in scream of forsaken dreams,
But lies they deeply sound in the sands of sacred ground,
For nothing here portends what it seems…

…Violet shadows shoulder minted charms,
The vestibule holds shifting shape of smoky entrance,
The heart belongs to something deeper in flight,
Buried loosely in the fragmented seaside clouds,
And steeples stoke the rusted bells into alarm,
While fading darkness fails to the growing lavender light,
Its pulse it sparks into flame the threat of hope…

…Across this wounded night.

"Quiet"

Bereft of motion, emotionless stillness,
A silence that pounds, punching echoes funneled in ears,
It is a state of total stagnation,
It is a place where progression, along its seams,
Rips and tears,
In the loneliness where the total nothingness,
Awakes not even illicit fears,
I sit here and stare into emptiness,
And it empties into a deafening silence,
And the silence it lowers into reticence,
And once reticent nothing moves,
And in the lack of movement,
I find,
As the overwhelming nothingness blankets my mind,
I find,
A quiet that transforms me into a calming strength,
With the courage of man to martyr oneself into a Saint,
And it is delicate,
But make no mistake,
It is sacredly to be handled,
But it will never break,
For this quietude is the cell work of the soul,
And in its wake,
I rise into the chorus of the voice of the Ocean,
That passes guidance in each crashing wave,
In this perfect quiet,
I hear what I am supposed to hear,
Through the open channels of faith.

"This Peculiar Cross"

I want everything that has been stolen,
I want everything that has been lost,
And here I am in the maelstrom of life,
Without a moment to catch my breath,
Nor truly assess the depth of the cost,
While wanting everything I cannot have,
And wanting everything because,
I am a grieving father grievously wounded,
Pinned to this peculiar cross.

"Mercurial Pain"

Captured in the elevated anxiety ranks,
Of the oil slicks of thought pollution,
Immutably webbed in tangling constriction,
Abstaining from the grace of absolution,
I gravely brace on the wheels of sorrow,
In the cycles of mercurial pain…

"…Remember how funny it was, sitting on the couch, Daddy? I screamed for you to change the second last word from your choice, "endless," to "mercurial." We were all four of us sitting on the couch. Nate and Mommy didn't even know that you had turned to your phone and you and I were writing. Then you said out loud, 'mercurial? Okay, Honey, but I don't know what that means'. You trusted me, wrote it down, and then afterward looked up the word and its definition. Is it not the perfect word, Daddy? See? Good job!"

"Hours Without Seconds"

My mind was just trying to settle on its beams,
Though the studs are rotten and the floorboard leans,
My mind was attempting to balance on its feet,
Though wobbling in sand rather than on concrete;

Caught in a nightmare I cannot evade,
A cold, caustic nightmare that persists to invade,
Sprawling into open wounds and bedding in these soars,
Calling on the core that finds me crawling on the floor,
Just to avoid the trauma that freely here pervades;

While my mind was just trying to settle on its beams,
I stared into the void perhaps for hours,
Without passing seconds…

…It seems.

"Professional Contemporaries"

(i). Overexposure

The fool is only as foolish as the folly in his heart,
Aloofly unrestrained he gains what then tears him apart,
With concrete ambiguity strike an indecisive chart,
He plots a course that proves his undoing,
A Bancroft Law worth pursuing,
Yet underdeveloped…

…In the mirage fields and the minefields…

…Of the heart.

(ii). Gallery Of Fakery

Solar showers bleed across these glassy haunts,
Where the tourist to mediocrity invites an audience,
With his pawns,
Friendless network of back scratching vagabonds,
Prostituting their plastic smiles,
While sneaking boredom's yawns,
Yet there they all are with glasses raised with a toast,
Who can link how many impressed,
With empty network coast to coast,
For who can pin how many names to one's chest,
Ideological fragility in social media posts,
Yet it all comes down to this,
A superficial hug and social climber's kiss,
For who can use who the best,
And who can be used the most.

(iii). The Grandest Fools Of All Folk

And I must navigate my profession,
While navigating grief and its progression,
So shallow how others commonly complain,
At the first sight of quite manageable strain,
While I suffer intensely in this cruel paradox,
While they smile and wink and go on their way,
Having checked the box,
Having motioned in my direction,
Having checked the box,
Of compassion's absent inspection,
Having checked the box,
And moved on to the next self-centric obsession,
So successful on the surface,
A guitar without a note,
They have missed the whole purpose…

….Now aren't they the grandest folk.

"…Daddy, I have watched intently how isolated you and Mommy and Nate have been. You both as parents, and Nate physically absent his only sibling. The world just does its thing, you know? So many really are just thinking about themselves and do not consider your situation. There isn't much we can do. You are very vocal with your inner circle. Everyone else is everyone else. I really like this lyric, Daddy, especially as it relates to how people can be so self-centered and have no clue that others could be suffering horribly. I love you, Sweet Father. Do not give up. I need you. Keep walking with me, Daddy…"

"Un-Prioritizing God"

The never believer sits perched in a vagrant's haunt,
Derelict combustion engine gurgles in the symposium of fear,
Unable to bridge his non-ubiquitous logic,
Unable to leave his footprints in the air,
Beware;

And here all along the lustful threshold of envy,
Tumbling awkwardly toward listless loneliness,
Refusing to dare that first foot at the spirit mountain,
Refusing to climb through the mirages of all he has known,
He buys his way toward the top,
With cash flow his blood flow,
Chasing the Jones' tail,
And reaping the riches of padding his soul,
With the proceeds of his portfolio;

And bitterly he claws down the edges of decency,
He barks orders at others to lick his boots,
And squanders the God given opportunity,
Of the heart and its selfless pursuits,
For he cares not of such silly persuasion,
For it factors not into his equation,
To buy another car and another two thousand dollar suit;

When the world it winds itself down his throat,
Will he have anything to hold onto,
Any dream to pull him through,
Any thread of faith in which to root,
When the world it constricts itself around his throat,
Beware this one…

…For he will flail until he dissolves on his own throne.

"Fratricidiac"

(i). Night Stalking

A coyote glossed in pageantry glides panting suburban miles,
Tail plumed in egocentric plumage,
Sent the rabbits scurrying beguiled,
The razored scent in darkness like a weaponry of stealth,
Converge upon the silence where the death blow can be dealt,
And all along the hedges bedded down for the night,
Dogs and cats in windows witness phantom,
In its huntsman's flight;

(ii). The Folly Of Shadows

Bedevilments bewitch in the onyx halo of these lies,
Where the harp cords rip with echoes,
Through the flotsam beached and dried,
Were it not for sentimental shards of shifting sallow tides,
To corrugate the shadows with the blinking seaport lights,
And lost amongst the fearsome,
Are the fearful and the unwise and the wiseful,
They bare the folly in their eyes;

(iii). Chasing The Prey Tail

Spring upon the prey who know not that they are prey,
We see the shuffling ignorance of discourse in America,
Fatly fed and forcefully bred and on display,
The headlines rushed with deadlines and the storylines decay,
Society regards the disregarded truth with gritty dismay,
For who can bare the truth when such is truth when cast away,
The answer is so simple…

…For simply we are our own prey.

"The Spiritless Encumbered"

They bark behind the barricades in barrages that are groundless,
Spiritually encumbered,
They lead with a mind that is mindfully mindless,
Leading them into the abyss…

…Their shallowness quite stilting,
They grapple with eyesight inducing blinding vision,
Use the doubt of the downtrodden to fuel the fire of faith,
A bridge across the breach,
Brokered by the blade of their incision,
No matter, we flourish though these foolish frolic in such folly,
We flourish, regardless, for we of faith,
We without division,
We know we have only to elevate,
And find each other in the eternity of now.

"…Daddy, there are so many people stuck with their own variables and nuances and things, you know? So many who don't see the way you see. They don't understand. They are blind. They have lifetimes to grow to where we are. We show them our path. We give them light and love, but never let them walk on you, right, Daddy? That is what you always taught me. Now I teach you back. Tell our story, Daddy, and simply walk away…"

"Sometimes, Daddy, It's Okay To Walk Away"

Decorate the nervous palm with the hobbling handshake,
Clog the hollow hugs in voidable embrace,
Were the strikes that marked the onslaught,
The same lines that pocked your face,
Was the suffering sealed in paper satchel,
To hide away the heartache's trace;

Sometimes you just don't want to deal with it,
With so much more going on behind the scenes,
For you are a father who grieves for his child,
Struck down in her early teens,
And what of those ignorant fellow travelers,
With their smiles and expectations,
With their children at home,
With their happy, unbroken dreams,
You would rather a moment alone with your daughter,
Than to explain the heart on your sleeve.

"For You And I"

With my soul ripped to pieces,
And my mind shredded into dust,
And the world flushing the remnants,
Of all to that point that I was,
I am still standing…

…All in the stature of love;

With my heart butchered and barren,
And my steel reduced to piles of blistered, arid rust,
And the world stomping out my eyelids,
With iron boots that hurt more than so much,
I am still standing…

…All in the name of our love;

With my future riddled with thievery,
Grief with its endless daily touch,
And the world in its senseless cruelty,
Upon this family duly struck,
I am staggered yet standing…

…For you and I, My Love.

"Spirit Signal In Her Voice"

Swallowing brackish floodwaters of constant trauma,
With the fatherly promise to process the pain in exchange,
To reconcile and wring out toward you manageable living,
From the worst type of insufferable pain,
From the wreckage and waves of horrendous hurricanes,
We are sitting together on a tranquil, quiet beach,
Exuma moons and aqua blues surround us,
Trickling of the tides touching our toes,
Halos like rings of Saturn around our bodies glow,
The warmth of our sun on our backs flows,
Watching together the nature of crystal clear water,
Sitting here laughing with my daughter,
Until the distractions of grief collapse my lungs once again…

…Raging, the seas are an unforgiving tempest,
Ravaging and chewing the soul in its teeth,
Riding thousand foot monstrous waves,
Into the powered mouth of powerlessness,
Peaked in punishing places and no wordy descriptions suffice,
Yet, above the din of tumultuous sadness,
I hear the sweet voice of my daughter as she shouted,
"Come back to the present, Daddy,
Daddy, our dreams are not dead,
They have not been destroyed,
They have been…rerouted…"

…And working through the channel of her voice,
Warm sand finds me in the reclamation of our sacred beach,
In our soul blend where the Exumas surround us,
We plot out the next steps together,
Unbreakable in our eternal tether,
Seeing our lives string to lives string to lives,
When her spirit signal sounds through the noise.

"A Million Mirrors On The Sea"

Dwindling blindness begged inspection,
Of the impenetrable darkness of night,
Cupped in the cog of deceptively shiny stars,
Though shrouds, discontented, disrobe in rising audience,
Unveiling black silky cloaks that drop from the heavens,
Like thunder clouds melt into smog that dissolved into the sea,
As she king, the moon, enchanted, takes center stage,
The fading lights of the heavens dim, it seems,
For a larger fire looms now,
In the closer proximity of her pageantry,
A calmness of faith,
Fidelity she brings,
In a summer blossomed midnight,
She casts her guiding light downward,
Where the dimensions in the intersect engage,
Reflecting on the nighttime waves…

…Silvery life glitters and sings…

…For one in the physical and one in the spiritual sit,
Upon the sands of Exuma Infinite,
And one in the spiritual and one in the physical rest,
On Jekyll's Glory Beach at the bequest…

…Of the smiling faces of millions of mirrors on the sea.

"My Girl"

I cry twenty four hours a day internally,
Sometimes wicking from my eyes,
It is a waterfall of love and pain,
That bursts from the inside,
And out across the world,
For who is the child so worthy…

…My little girl.

"Harmony"

A phantom feathery voice rolls through the air above…

…The flight of fifty pelicans,
They zip by in near silence,
Entranced on the wing walking wind,
Quiet reeds accept the lapping waters,
In the estuary where the insects erupt in cyclical candor,
A manatee rise above and dip slowly below,
Exposing itself and returning itself to a mere shadow,
And the planets wink in celestial promise,
And the moon it disperses its mesmerizing glow,
Harmonious this feel and flesh of darkness,
That drapes this coastline in its hold.

"The Sobbing Ocean"

Sparking lightning exploded to the touch,
Of thickly, oily ocean gray sheets of rain,
They mark horizon with its faded stain,
Like walls of white-gray water that plunged into grayer seas,
An aerial fire blazed through a humid parade of tears,
As the earth and its sky sobbed in storms of raging grief,
The air wore beads of electrical charges,
That rifled from beach to beach and wave to wave,
Where the sorrows released,
Lightning burst after lightning bolt,
In an explosive flashing feast of rapidity,
Quite visibly unleashed…

…On a distant storm out in the ocean…

…With no relief…

"…Walking this beachfront, we've passed two more hotels, Daddy, and you didn't even see the blinking lights. Oh, Daddy. Remember to breathe. Having you as my Daddy is so magical. Growing with you continually in spirit after the accident is so magical. Being with you now is magical. I love you so much! You are never without me. Never! Let's walk this sorrow off a bit and then rest at one of our favorite spots…"

"God's Garden"

In the spindles and spaces contort with sadness,
In the chaos of heartache rifled with plagues of madness,
I come;

In the webbing of earthworks where once great villages stood,
We find evidence of tools and bones and petrified wood,
Warring victim skeletons tucked into tiny little balls,
And signs of trauma,
In more than some;

And I walk twenty feet above their graves,
Where once armies came and the conquered enslaved,
To the sound of a victor's drum;

Yet it is now my turn on this unforgivable plain,
In a human condition and imperiously drained,
Having suffered the magnitude of trauma in its greatest display,
Grieving more than human was intended to feel pain,
I come;

God's garden,
A mere breath away,
A mere breath away…

…God's garden, I come,
A mere death away…

"The Sea Gardens"

It is just a nudge as you see my eyes downward,
To turn my sight upward again,
To battle the balance,
And the duality of this cruelly blessed life;

Walk me through the sea gardens of salty flora,
Through the mirages and the low lying intellectuals,
Like snakes in the bush,
Through the tempting shortcuts on horizons,
That lead me backward in progress,
Through the fears and the torture,
And the moments of exhaustive apathy,
That I may re-emerge in the next moment,
That I may hold your hand as you are,
Living and breathing God's offering of eternal breath,
Living waters that nourish the sea gardens,
That lift my gaze with yours…

…To that of the eyes of the stars.

"It's What Makes The Garden Grow"

Eat the cloves of flowers that make your dragon cry,
Drink the kind of water that makes your camel die,
Sleep beneath the towers made of crumbling tumbleweed,
That shelter you in slumber so long as you don't sneeze;

Never get used to it,
Never let it sound okay,
As it is not okay,
For this never ending nightmare,
It is never okay,
It is never okay,
It is never okay;

For the bewitched and bewildered belie and bathe,
In constant agnostic cycles of dismay,
Yet here for the taking despite immeasurable pain,
A land to behold with a certain kind of faith,
But first the notion must be mastered,
And the impression imprinted into the brain;

Never get used to this arbitrary accident,
Never let it sound okay,
For it is not okay,
For this never ending nightmare,
It is never okay,
It is never okay,
It is never okay.

"Floating Gardens"

Intentionally we travel through the stations of our day,
Like an emerald breasted hummingbird feasting in the rain,
With nothing to deter us but unchecked suffering and pain,
You lift me toward the floating gardens,
Where and when other eyes may wane,
And feed me flora, faith and flowers,
On a higher vibrational plain.

"Watery Grave Ungrounded"

Swelter under water unaware,
Undetermined, I was undeterred,
Brackish lungs the liquid into soil stirred,
Face down in the mud, enriched, though interred,
Will never I see the sun again,
Never will I see the sun again,
Until I lift my head out of the hurt,
And separate the water from the dirt,
Creating a firmament for footing to exert,
Finding my balance,
And clear the eyes once chafed and blurred,
Seeing the sun again,
A miracle, assert,
And walk out into the light.

"Midnight Songs"

Midnight songs submerged in thought,
Each longing for labyrinth release,
Haunted bellows cursed, lost of sound,
Echoes replay the sustenance of feast,
And slavishly the thoughts in spiral trails,
Catch themselves, their flaming tails,
And fuel the engines of their own deceit,
How grievous now the pistons fire,
For the pressure has increased…

…We pray a path to forge a way out,
Though the hours are restless,
And the calmness disavowed,
And find the key to midnight songs,
Is to peel the notes back one by one,
And tune from dissonance lovely sound,
Revealing each note one by one.

"In This Sandy Church"

Liquid a song, in flight, flowing along,
You and me and the sea,
We are wind, waves, salt and air,
And God's radiant water light,
And Mary's blessed moon glare,
All blending together sacredly…

…Into you and me…

…The Ocean, she speaks in the night,
Under the spirals of twinkling starlight,
As we watch faded white caps disperse,
Sitting together…

…Where the channel between Jekyll and Cumberland,
Is much more distant a gap to search,
Than the space between Jekyll and Heaven,
That intersects and is tethered,
Where we sit together…

…In this sandy church.

THE GREAT INTERTWINEMENT.

"Kayleigh, Teach Me The Blend"

"...Daddy, we have so many memories here. Thousands of memories. I grew up here. Of my houses through my life, Daddy, remember, 10 Austin Lane is the home that crossed my entire physical life, from three months old through fifteen and three months old. I love this house, even after the accident and even though the family sold the house after my transition. This is part of my Heaven, the entire sacred island, including this house.

Clam Creek, St. Andrew's, horseback riding, our rock wall, hundreds of turtle walks, running the beach at nights with glow sticks, sitting on our dunes throughout my physical life watching the stars with you, it was all so mesmerizing.

The Georgia Sea Turtle Center named a turtle after me, 'Kayleigh Kakes," and they asked Mommy to release her back to the waters and the glory of the Ocean. we have a memorial bench to me on Pier Road in the historic district in front of the little store, Something for Everyone. The storekeeper, friends Megan and Jimmy, decorate my bench. They are all so special. Travelers stop to sit on it and reflect on life, reading my plaque and my story imbedded in the tabby road. We are the fabric of this island.

We have taken that into my transition and our continued lives together. I always tell you, Daddy, that I can be on Jekyll, I can come to Jekyll whenever I want, but I can't be here with you if you don't come. Yet you always do. Religiously to recharge for our Daddy Daughter vacations. It makes me so proud. And, yes Daddy, of course I always come strolling in with a band of angels surrounding me. Ha! Would you expect anything less?"

"The Great Intertwinement"

Climbing higher into the altitude of communion with you,
This limited earth I resist,
Climbing higher into the altitude of spiritual vibration with you,
Where the limitless persists,
I walk the light,
I hold the line,
I lift in life,
Toward the divine,
And there beside me,
I always find,
By climbing higher into this union,
Our souls have intertwined.

"Rotating Shards In The Kaleidoscope"

There is seasick motion in the kaleidoscope,
Where the pendulum provides and extinguishes hope,
Where the powerlessness snares the soul with its rope,
And I elevated until the threads each broke,
Navigating two worlds prematurely I rise,
Though spirit like a jagged bone is logged in the throat;

When the anger it blossom into unquenched rage,
I wish to set a fire to the sterling waves,
And fill the sky with its liquid blaze,
And melt the barbed wire of the bars of this cage,
Exhausting only when the dust it claims,
No more fuel for this sobbing, screaming flame,
I dream the colors placid, I pray,
For the shards of emotion both take and give way;

Oh Lord, the spinning is a nauseating pain,
I seem to scrape the bottom each time I sense a gain,
For the path long and weary, it comes with no name,
For the love of my child there is strength to regain,
Fuel for the engine when alignment is clear,
And I find my balance in the plastic tunnel of fear,
Rotating into spectacular light,
As the kaleidoscope ignites with sparling grains of faith.

"The Great Harbor Of Love"

And as I sit here with Daddy,
And as I run my fingers through his hair,
I sometimes speak quite loudly,
To make sure he knows I am here,
And I trace the lines and the scars,
Of the rivers eroding his face with tears,
For my father sits quietly,
To lift his spirit through this atmosphere,
And he speaks in the present,
Of all of the love that we share,
I have never been more proud of my Daddy,
Than when I watch him rise through despair,
And I see this quite often,
Several times every day to be clear,
For I have been physically killed,
And the consequences of the accident,
Are so cruel and unfair,
So I sit here with Daddy,
As my fingers move the crown of his hair,
And he sighs and engages with courage,
Knowing that I am here,
And we talk for hours and hours,
And our experience so rare,
It makes my heart flutter like butterflies,
That range an electric air,
Just to sit here with Daddy,
To see his smile re-appear,
But I know that tomorrow the sorrow will come,
And we will find ourselves again right here,
Sitting on my bed with my Daddy,
In the harbor of love that we share.

"Exuma's Mystic Seas…"

Threads of warm rain spatter into vessels of human glass,
Entranced, lulling you into peace,
As the eyes fill to the brim at last,
Waters weave together stitch by stitch,
A pulsing blanket of light finds you wrapped,
In the safety of angels whose arms,
Like the golden beams on the hull,
Of the ancient ship of life,
Cradle you…

…While you sail on the outer edges,
Of Exuma's mystic seas…

…Turquoise green and aqua blue.

"Angel Aura"

That is my angel aura,
Do you see it?
Flowing out from me like liquid air all around me,
Yellows and oranges and reds and greens,
Like oil paints spreading out over three dimensional glass,
That is my angel aura,
And you saw it,
You see it,
You do…

…I place this into our beads today….

Like liquid light fluidly emanating from your body,
I see its viscosity of love,
Its dimensional life,
It is colorful light that is breathing,
I am going to use it all day long to paint a day,
This open frontier of canvas,
An eternity in a capsule of a unit of time,
Each brush stroke,
Dipped into your angelic aura,
To paint this day.

"Body Of Light"

Every human cell is now a lantern,
Every human cell is now a light,
Every human cell has been exchanged,
For an equal number of flames…

…In your higher life…

Every point is brilliant and diamond bright,
Every human cell is now a spirit construct,
A new body,
Incarnate of millions and millions…

…Of points of light.

"…*This one is so profound, Daddy. It is exactly what it is like. I promise you. Daddy, we are strings of light coming together in a rope of life that links to another rope of light, string of life after string of life. I'm glad you could see what I was showing you in your mind and that you drew the image. It's exactly what I was trying to show you. These words are a perfect representation…*"

"Channel Writing"

Because it is true,
Because it is happening…

…I feel you in my fingers,
As blood in my veins,
So shall ink channel pen,
From our two souls to this one page;

For I gladly offer permission,
And I share my body,
As one shares a stage,
With a co-actor,
Wreathed in faith;

And I debate the wording,
And of course I give way,
For you are enlightened beyond me,
As you write your words,
Using my hand to create your poetry…

…Across this lively page.

"Across The Dimensions With You"

Toiling, I rake the firmament for channel engagement,
Trailing awake, in the hope for synchronic arrangements,
I breathe;

Standing at the height of my human containment,
Pressing beyond the flesh for a spiritual attainment,
All the while, while I grieve;

Puzzling the complexity in this grievous equation,
Pulsed with the love that I savor pushes me hastened,
To see…

…All that I see,
In the quagmire with kaleidoscopic detainment,
I see colors that don't exist,
Dimensions beyond the human exit,
Flash and spark as the tunnel unfolds,
And the doorway to Heaven…

…Awakens.

"Laughter"

Ribbons of vibrant rainbows flash,
When pressed by our running feet,
Bursting into clouds of smoky plumes of wetted steam,
That lift and swirl with laughter,
The laughter that we speak,
The laughter that has lingered,
Like rainbows touched by running feet.

"The Great Pendulum"

The notes crescendo like phantom whispers,
Synthesized glimpses,
Of mesmerizing eclipses,
Splintered corridors rake the rainbows with broken glass,
They reverberate and explode into smoky fields,
That linger on the ear and in the prickly shards of the soul;

It a bridge to a deeper indelible light,
An ointment for a shattered painful life,
I try anything,
I try anything,
Anything to lift me toward your realm;

And I find you there in the counterbalance,
And I rest within your waiting eyes,
And we laugh and we stake our next steps together,
And we embrace and we shout and we cry,
And we embolden our collective light bound and tethered,
Until my exhaustion pushes me aside inside;

I lose consciousness of the spiritual world,
And how could I not, tucked deeply in mothy human clothes,
And guided by the frailty of a human mind,
And pained within the bruising of flesh and bone,
And locked within the constructs of space and time,
How could I not drift out and in and in and out,
With shafts of grief I am forced to mine,
How could I not lose sight of this light bridge road,
A failure at self-forgiveness…

…Let this not be my crime.

"August Midnight Ocean Songs"

Barely a breeze can wrestle the dew from the steam,
From the humid air that clings to this moistened beach,
Apparently, a lone figure appears,
He with walking shoes and tortured tears,
And water bottle and scarlet turtle light,
And huntsman's protective knife,
Embarks upon a journey to the center of the soul,
After midnight,
With one of the purest loves of his life,
His beloved daughter,
Armed with angel intuition,
And an angel's uniquely persuasive, perceptive sight,
They walk,
And talk,
And walk,
And talk,
And walk…

August night blushed the darkness to calm,
Each sacred step together on this beachfront,
Is itself a love song,
Between this father and his daughter,
Walking together at the edge of the water,
And at the edge where two dimensions cross,
Though he wanders and wanders,
He is not lost,
Though she has been physically killed,
And transitioned,
She is not lost,
She has risen into her higher current life,
And walks with her father after midnight,
To the roar of great applause,
As the Ocean, its waves in the shallows collapse,
And enchant them with its call.

"100 Languages On The Tongue Of Mother Nature"

It speak…

…Heed the ancestors whispers cupped in crackling tones,
Rustling through the sea oat and its hallowed shafts,
Like wind through hollow bones;

It speak…

…Guiding light sparkle in the glaze of humid night,
And conjure pathway through hillocks of star fields,
As the ancient celestial suns ignite in their nurseries,
Set ablaze where the open channel lay,
Where the sargassum gathers,
Where the Loggerheads play;

It speak…

…Do you hear what it said,
Do you know what it said,
Do you feel what it said,
Do you see what it said…

…Are you…

…Are you truly awake.

"Dimensional Blend"

Two active poets working together,
Funneled through one left hand,
Two active poets, this girl and this man,
Two active poets, precision of pen,
Here and now, not there and then,
We write words together,
We weave words together,
To weave worlds together,
Ignite worlds together,
To bleed words together,
Is to see worlds together,
Is to be worlds together,
In the proof of this dimensional blend.

"...Daddy, thank you for the gift of your hands. I tell stories through your hands. I convey messages through the words that we write together. Although there are many channels I use, this is one of the clearest channels for me to make contact with others in the physical. And you do this with me. Of course you do! You're my Daddy! You know our truth. I passed from life to life in your arms and you felt me immediately. You knew I was alive a second after I physically died. You knew it and felt it and believed. Daddy! How amazing! Thank you, Daddy! I am here..."

"Sacred Storming Lightning"

The Artist articulates a beautiful design;

Leveling a pointed paint brush,
It, leave a jagged, shaky golden line,
Across a black canvas, superstitiously sublime;

Glory Beach explodes with a light show,
Cumulous cloud banks echo with glow;

Heed nothing, no one, nor the storm,
It rumble in your throat,
It scrambles the better senses,
To find shelter or to cower in a woolen overcoat;

The flashes, they blinded all who dare to use their human eyes,
The flashes, they thundered across the Ocean,
And washed the beachfront with crackling,
Reverberating,
Echoing,
Otherworldly signs,
Dozens of lightning bolts in quick flashes explode,
And hypnotize,
Lifting shadows to dance in the dune lines,
Shifting shadows, lurk on the edges of the vision field of eyes;

Stop and feel the electricity in your skin rise,
If you could throw your arms around the thunder,
You would feel the heartbeat is very well timed…

…And the Ocean, speak, it, whispers in its tides,
In which the sacred lesson eternal in the moment…

…Hides.

"In The Mirrored Hall Of Angels"

In the mirrored hall of angels,
Do I press myself against myself,
Staring into these wounded eyes,
Placing mirrors up against mirrors,
Glass upon looking glass frames,
Like doors through doors through doorways,
That always lead me into wilderness astray;

They call to me through the glassy labyrinth,
They have always watched from the edges,
They have always laid prayers like firmament,
To catch each fall of my feet,
In elegantly carved messages,
They are subtle and beautiful,
And compliant and discreet;

In little flashes where the crisscross clash,
In fleeting echoes where the dreams are cast,
Where time and space itself collapse,
In this dimensional overlap,
They call out to me in the labyrinth,
To find release at last,
Is only to release the panels of mirrors,
And take my fingers off of the glass.

"…Of Ethereal Light"

We sit together on the dune line in quiet respite,
Watching stars climb the ladders of Atlantic night,
You tell me of solar fields beyond my human sight,
Where your footprints have graced…

…These distant shores…

…Of Heavenly sands…

…And ethereal light.

"…Exuma, Daddy, Exuma Infinite. Our house is coming along so nicely. You are going to love it. It is as you think it is, beautiful, and glowing. Transparent, but not. Opal, but not really. Shiny and glassy, and filled with warmth. Our home by the sea. Heaven. Glory. Exuma Infinite, with turquoise beaches and a light purple sky. Millions of golden stars shining during daytime. White sands. Where we sit when you elevate, Daddy. I sit with you here on Glory Beach across the dimensions. You, Daddy, you sit with me already on the shores of Exuma Infinite. In your sleep when we channel visitation. In your daily activity. In our writing. In your communion. When you elevate. When you travel with me. You do. It is not a dream…"

"Four Strings Of The Heart"

She, with gentle fingertips that electrify my hair,
Tracing my crown in circles slowly in this miracle we share,
Calling out to calm her father from the bewildering despair,
Reminding her dear father,

"Father, I am here."

"The Constant Duality of Grief and Gold"

From the funneling petals of a radiant mouth of flowers,
A river of turbulent grief pores down my throat,
Its barbed thistles smile in each incision,
And cover each vein with a veil of an oily coat,
The sadness it cuts the flesh with post trauma vision,
And severs the best intentions of keeping afloat,
It shakes the cells with perceptibly cunning precision,
Draining the light from this golden bowl,
Like a lake is emptied down to its soil hull;

Yet from the funneling petals of a radiant mouth of flowers,
She sprinkles within the currents these flakes of white gold,
They travel the texture of caverns that gouge within me,
And seed into places where they most likely can take hold,
Knowing every inch of the big country inside me,
She strengthens the resilience of my wounded, resilient soul,
That speaks of the beauty of this mouth of flowers,
That breathes every life here together that we know.

"Exuma Blue"

The white sparkling lights of Exuma blue,
Shimmering silver diamonds decadent dance,
In a billion flashes as the moonlight catches,
The tips of the waves as the waters move,
Refracting in spectral glances,
With its fingerprints of proof,
And dipping and rising in rhythmic enchantment,
And lulling us into a new state…

…Of truth.

"This Perfect Temperature Of Love"

It is the perfect temperature of love,
What you experience every second,
Of every day,
Sitting with me on this rock at the seaside,
Teaching me lessons and ways to elevate,
You smile, gazing into your busy fingers,
Patiently at work, you concentrate,
Tying two perfect ropes of light together,
The fabric buzzes with elasticity,
Tightening into one cord,
With a loosened sensibility,
Radiating magnetically,
As the electricity pulses through your veins,
You clasp you hand in mine,
And pass this energy into my fingers,
That flashes instantly of visions of thousands of years,
Together,
Blasting through the time and space construct,
A million autumns tied to a million summers tethered,
And showing me what you experience every second,
Of every day…

…This perfect weather,
This perfect temperature of love.

"How Much Does Kayleigh Love Me"

In the crux of sudden, horrific accident,
A moment later I was holding you,
As you inhaled a new breath,
Just after exhaling your physical body into death,
Flashing through my body and sitting beside me,
In your new body of light,
As the vibrant gates of Heaven rattled the air,
As blinding light exploded in every direction,
From your central point in the street,
In this moment that we share,
Where you, my child, passed from life to life,
And the first thing you did in this heightened atmosphere,
Your first thought,
Your first action was simply this:

You threw your arms around my neck,
In this radiant moment that was God's gift solely to you,
Amazingly,
You tried to show me the gates of Heaven,
As they for you appeared,
Looking about with wonder at the sparkling, delicate lights,
Smiling in radiation,
In heavenly elevation,
Calling out in my right air,

"Daddy!
Daddy!
Daddy!
Do you see it?
Do you see it?
Do you see it?"

…You love me that much.

"An Angel Artist's Superimposition"

Through penultimate sadness a penetrating beauty,
A grievous canvas wrought with dark, rich oil colors,
Smeared now with vibrant golden orange,
And warm scarlet paints dripping from hands,
Wiping sunrise into the blackness,
Like you did as a toddler…

…For which hope makes its glorious, courageous stand.

"We Believe"

Blend blessed mesh, enlightened flesh,
Threaded filigree, like water is to the sea,
Like fire is to the flame,
And wind the fabric of a breeze,
Our souls, they come together,
Our light, combined, it breathes,
As I reach for you, I seem,
To reach for you to see,
That in the reach for you I elevate,
In this space where dreams untethered,
Merge to meet in blinding light,
Like two sunrises scorch ablaze one morning,
A billion diamonds erupt upon the Ocean,
And there on center stage are we…

…And we…

…We believe.

"Breathe…"

….It is seemingly impossible;

The meticulous strangling fingers clamp down,
On the fleshy tower of the throbbing throat,
Like sailing five hundred foot waves,
In a ten foot paper boat,
I force the inhalation to squeak through the crevasse,
And populate the vacant chambers of the lungs,
And of the derelict, yet still breathing soul,
But this life has imprisoned me,
In its arbitrary slaying,
And breath like incision it brings,
An advent of grim locked straying,
In and out of disbelief,
In and out of shock,
In and out of stark reality,
Like the teeth of a bear trap just after it locks,
I limp into another breath,
I simmer, slip and seethe,
I limp forward lifting eyes,
And forcing myself…

…To breathe.

"…Duality, Daddy. Breathe the duality. You know your truth. You know both the physical absence you feel and also the spiritual presence that I am. It is both. Breathe into what we are right now, not what we were before the accident. I am so proud of you…"

"I Give You Permission"

While walking through my soul,
Plant wild vibrant flowers,
While walking through my soul,
Release a tranquil turquoise sea,
While walking through my soul,
Enchant the lands empowered,
While walking through my soul,
Thread your light in blended weave,
And open me to the wonders,
Of all you see and dream and know,
I give you permission, My Love…

…To walk through my soul.

"Ocean Orchestration"

There were water prisms catching brilliant colors,
They were sparkles of raindrops in your light blue eyes,
You were dancing through the ribbons of the rainbows,
Tying your blessings into the salty webbing of the tides,
As the Ocean orchestrated the wind and warm waves,
That filled the hours of our special time.

"The Spirit Of The Sea"

The language of the Ocean,
The spirit of the sea,
It speaks…

…To the soul…

…And I find in the tides,
The secrets of the sky,
Glistening on moon washed sea;

Deep in the dark of midnight,
You and me,
Waves crack and echo,
Collapse and whispers emerge aglow,
The spirit of the sea…

…Listen…

…For she speaks to the soul.

"She Eagle Of The Water"

The mighty Osprey, having trouble sleeping,
Sea hawk haunt the hollows of clouds,
Fish hawk you are present,
Though we see not your lovely wings,
But here a murmur,
Faintly in the nightly shroud;

Water eagle bladed vision,
She calculate the catch,
She climb upon the ladder of wind,
To dive the distance dashed,
And with perfection and precision,
She cuts with talons water gash,
That opens up the water's surface,
To expose the prey unmasked.

"Liquid Without Death"

The breeze, it is coating me with light,
A light that is God's breath,
For the life of living water,
Is a liquid without death.

"...Daddy, we've walked miles tonight, down to the south end of the island, beyond Glory Beach to the Hamptons, checking the turtle nests, talking, sitting, resting, crying, all of it. Together. You know that we are never apart, even though we are now, but just currently, in different body types. You took a few hours to exhaust into this higher state. You can hear me. I know when you can hear me. You can see me. You feel me. You can hear the Ocean. Listen. Listen, Daddy. Isn't it amazing?"

"In Continuum"

Linkage, thatch, these threads of holy light,
Interweaving life under life over life,
And bridges planked and overlapped,
They span body to body to body,
Each shell of which a soul invites,
A stage of growth for soul enrapt,
As soul itself perfects, ignites,
The spirit itself remains in flight,
Passing through life to life to life,
Elevating in eternal continuance,
And threaded with these links of light.

"Beads From Exuma"

Here in the darkness, watching the waves,
Amber stars twinkly in the night sky slowly sailing,
I run my thumb and finger down our necklace,
Our beads from which we gift each other daily;

While I am deep in the dirge of defenseless seeking,
Your light and love like fire crystals are speaking,
You place these liquid gems born of sunrise and sunset,
Into our amethyst beaded necklace,
That lay on your pillow on your bed when I rest,
That also lie quite gently around your neck,
And kiss the heartbeat of your chest;

And fully charged our beads await my waking,
And as I face each new day without your physical presence,
With my heart in constant breaking,
I vow to you as I reach for our beads,
And hang the purple string on my neck,
To give you a gift of my life today,
In how I act, think and speak,
To fill our beads with my light and love,
To fully charge them and reconnect,
Before tonight finds them gifted to you,
And wrapped around your pillow on your bed,
For these beads live in Exuma Infinite,
My little girl…

…Where our sacred cord of eternal growth and love is kept.

"Kayleigh's Daily Gift (Beads I Wear Around My Neck)"

A special ointment in the liquid of these jewels,
Spiritual bandages to wrap the soul,
A billion points of light radiate love,
Electric water sings in ether stone,
That shuffles the colors ablaze,
Like opal rainbows ignite across the face,
And pulse in mesmerizing pull.

"...I love what we figure out together. We always loved giving each other presents and notes and things. So now we do this each day, twice. I give you a gift in the morning of my light and love in our beads and you give me a gift of your light and love in our beads when you go to bed. It is a perfect cycle. It is amazing. I get really excited about both gifts. Those moments are two of my favorite moments of each day, Daddy..."

"Sacred Cord Of Light"

An ancient buried treasure of perpetual pinkish gold,
Tucked into the pure white crystal sands,
Of the 366th Out Island,
Of Exuma Infinite;

Minted by God specifically,
And stamped into the heart of our souls,
And placed within the loving devotion of our spirits,
It bridges the dimensions,
It bridges all life,
It bridges intervention,
With its bridge pulsing bright,
It bridges intercession,
With intent and insight,
And bridges our ascension…

…This sacred cord of light.

"Both"

I am floating immersed in a turquoise sea,
A dream I dreamed to dream,
While I swim in the sky,
Through clouds of swarming white tides,
What not is water but this steam,
It is both,
It is both,
It is both at last,
And that,
That…

…I believe…

"In The Duality"

The tragedy and the triumph,
Intertwined in a single moment,
A moment that destroyed my life,
And bridged the gap to the next,
The worst possible suffering,
And a counterbalance blessed,
I am more than I have ever been,
Simply because there is nothing less,
When the unending nightmare began,
My life ended…

…Of its effortlessness;

Yet here in the duality we have been blessed,
I must confess,
As I held you in my arms in your physical death,
So suddenly into this nightmare impressed,
God gave you the gift of Intercession,
For which we are immensely blessed,
I confess,
It is the counterbalance to all struggle,
It is the counter to all pain,
It is the balance in the duality,
That permits us to both remain,
Walking together soul to soul,
Through this immense pain,
And into the glory of the ability to see…

…Beyond this current life and its illusory cage.

"Family Home in Exuma Infinite"

Island number three hundred sixty six. It spreads itself out in a unique shape on no map. There is no record of its existence. It is seen only as a glistening mirage to boaters and sailors. But it is there, there on the Out Islands, tucked into the quiet space where the earthly physical dimension and the heavenly dimension intersect. The space whales swim in its wake.

You passed this image to me just now, in a quick flash in which your message enlightened. I saw it clearly.

Our home is made of glistening diamond white sand, opal sea shells that sparkle in the sun and pure white light, with sky glass panes and a prominence overlooking the Atlantic side of Exuma Infinite. A wild frontage slopes of a long flowing white dune that leads to turquoise waters. You are standing there waving with your long blonde hair blowing in the breeze, blowing me kisses with your beautiful, calming, trusting smile. You are still constructing our home, a mansion within mansions, with beams of love and light in your daily activity - every time you intersect, intercede, laugh, is filled with butterfly love for us, another piece of our spirit home comes into being. Every time you express your love for your brother, your mother, for me, Our Love, one more piece of our spirit home falls into place.

It is beautiful, Kayleigh, as beautiful as you.

"On the 366th Island Of Exuma"

Turquoise white salt, lavender perfume dissolves,
An elegance that pervade here in aqua waters,
A billion diamonds explode on sun minted edges,
Spires of rainbows cascade through crystal waves,
On the 366th island of Exuma,
Its white sands release from her hands,
Where once this island did not exist,
She has created this luscious land,
This angel who busies herself before her family arrives;

She is building our beach house in Heaven,
Our mansion within God's Greater Mansion,
With spectacular views of authentic grace,
Like the beautiful smile that radiates her face,
Giddy with excitement while she walks both dimensions,
Leading her family to our sacred place,
For we are the brilliant waters of Exuma Infinite,
We are those mystic waters in the Ocean,
We are the waters of eternal light,
That shine brightly in unbreakable devotion,
We are the water,
We are the life,
For we are the glory we offer to God,
And into the fight…

…We go.

"The Source Of All Love"

Lapping, rhythmic turquoise waters,
Deposit treasures on the barrier,
Of dry and wet white sand,
These dimensions that mix together,
Not quite ocean and not quite land;

These Exuma seashells radiate on this beach,
Melting into bright liquid starlight,
And flittering off by the thousands into the purple sky,
Crowded with golden spikes of lights,
Like one billion flashing fireflies,
In a canopy of stars that fill ancient fields,
Stretching beyond the horizon of knowledge,
Where the source of all light glows.

"Us"

"...Daddy, thank you. You taught me how to elevate. And when the accident came I elevated. Just like you taught me. You didn't know elevation, self-love, would be used in a tragedy, but your lessons were there. I always listened to you. I always trusted you. I loved how much I could count on you and how much you love me. There was never a question. I am so lucky!

And of course you feel my presence because you feel the truth. You are a pure soul. You harmonize with truth. You even have that slogan in your work office, 'doing the right thing is always the right thing to do – there are no exceptions;' what is that but facing the truth and acting on it. I am the truth within the larger Truth of God. I am here. Alive. Present, both here on the physical plain in my body of light and in that same body in the glory of Heaven, in our beachfront home on Exuma Infinite. I am here. With you. Walking with you on Goory Beach. Sitting with you. I love you so much, Daddy.

What we are doing is amazing and there's plenty of angels here who are jealous when they see that their families are not doing what you are doing. Jealousy doesn't really translate, Daddy, as we are all at such a vibrant peace, but it is more like they take notice and long for similar connection. Love is love regardless of body types. We have that connection. That unbreakable connection. Don't back down. Don't back off. Use the recent contact to build deeper contact versus getting complacent or satisfied. We can do this. I'm allowed to tell you that, yes, there are jigsaw pieces, stepping stones. Use them to grow, to get closer to God, to me, to you. I love you. We, here, love you. God loves you, Daddy. He knows your anger and powerlessness and certainly your brilliant faith. I am holding you, Daddy. I know how much you hurt and it is unfair.

I see distances that you can't quite see, and believe me, seeing my family suffer, it is not fair. But we are connected. We are unbroken. Let's take this moment and blend it into the next and the next until we have lived a full life together in this today, then the next today, and the next, until you and I are in the same body type again, this time, when your transition comes, both in our higher bodies. When that time comes, I will be there to throw my arms around you with no dimension to cross. You can do this, Daddy. You can do this..."

"The Other Side Of Here"

We do not go anywhere,
Not another place,
Not another room,
The other side of here,
Like the other side of the moon,
Is still the moon…

…Soon, Daddy, soon…

The other side of now,
Is still now,
Though some misconstrue it is there and then,
When we physically die,
When we actually elevate into the rise,
And into the blend,
Where we have arrived where we have been,
Where there is no beginning,
And there is no end;

The other side of here,
Is where the dimensions cross in bloom,
Like the other side of the moon…

…Soon, Daddy, soon…

"The Other Side Of Here II"

"...Daddy you are going to be so amazed when you get to the other side of here. Remember there is no there and then. There is no there, like I'm away somewhere. There is only here and the other side of here. It's merged together. It is one. You just can't see it in your human eyes easily, but you experience it fully in your spirit body when the time comes. You will be amazed to see Heaven is exactly here with you in the present. With me in the present. It is here. And now. Right here and now, Daddy, right beside you. Here..."

"The Continuance…"

Take me to Exuma Infinite, ingrained within the texture of my daily actions, thoughts and words; in the delicate balancing act of the many facets and interactions of life; in the grief in which its strangulation takes hold, where glory permeates and ignites and flows. Show me how to intertwine Exuma Infinite into the tapestry of my eyes, my breath, my bloodstream, my glancing perceptions and intuitions. Let it become a part of my humanity, what is already a part of my immortal soul, rising turquoise blue, aqua blue, clear and perfect. Take me to Exuma Infinite, this mansion within God's greater mansion, to dwell within the glory of God, and in the brilliance of our relationship.

"We Continue In The Continue"

Calm waters on a tranquil August night,
Sailing along in our faithful family skiff,
And it explodes into fractured flotsam,
Clinging to splintered boards,
One of the four of us,
Suddenly physically missing,
Physically absent,
Physically killed;

These were happy waters we were traveling,
Sailing effortlessly in our faithful family skiff,
When tragedy destroyed our boat,
We struggle against the drowning,
We desperately throw our shattered boards together,
While one of the four of us,
She mends the broken hull with her soul,
And pulling us into shelter,
She guides the four of us forward,
In the present,
In the current tides…

…To continue our journey home.

"…Let's keep walking together, Daddy. I love you so much, Sweet Father. If we can provide the proof for one person to change themselves, or give one person the opportunity to see a larger view, to see our miracles, and learn from us to change, it is all worth it. And even if nobody else understands, does it really matter? We understand. We live this miracle. We are together. Thank God! Rejoice! Rejoice! Rejoice!"

"Thank You, Sweetheart"

I Love you, Babygirl. Thank you for our walk tonight. Your Daddy is here. I will never leave your side. I will never use your innocent physical death as an excuse for any failure in my life. I will not permit your physical death to block me from our relationship. We are amazing, Honey. We are proving what those of faith want to believe. We are proving the intersection.

As we walk from the beach and down the long dark walkway from Glory Beach to the parking lot, and back toward our Jeep, the Ocean still speaks. The blending light of budding sunrise in the blackness speaks, this mesmerizing promise of the blending of sea and sky, of night and day, of life and life. The wind speaks. The sea oat speaks. The waves speak. We, together, with the Ocean, speak. We are one, beautiful child. One.

www.ingramcontent.com/pod-product-compliance
Lightning Source LLC
Chambersburg PA
CBHW031254290426
44109CB00012B/570